WB316

S0-BAE-442

DATE DUE

SCIENCE EVERYWHERE!

Backyard Bugs

The Best Start in Science

By Jenny Vaughan

New
Forest
Press

First published in North America in 2010 by New Forest Press,
PO Box 784, Mankato, MN 56002
www.newforestpress.com

TickTock project editor: Rob Cave
TickTock project designer: Trudi Webb

ISBN 978-1-84898-290-1
Library of Congress Control Number: 2010925586
Tracking number: nfp0002
Printed in the USA
9 8 7 6 5 4 3 2 1

Picture credits (t=top, b=bottom, c=center, l=left, r=right,
OFC=outside front cover, OBC=outside back cover):

Alamy: 9tl, 12br, 13t, 17tl, 17tr, 18b, 19tr, 21tr. Corbis: 7bl, 15c.
Saharadesertfox/wikimedia commons: 9tr. Science Photo Library: 6bl, 19l.
Shutterstock: OFC all, 1 all, 2, 3, 4-5 all, 6t, 6-7 main, 8-9 main, 9b, 10 all,
11c, 11b, 12l, 12tr, 12br, 13b, 14tl, 16 all, 17c, 17br, 17bl, 18t,
19cr, 19c, 20 all, 21tl, 21c, 21b, 22-23 all, 24 all, OBC all.

Contents

Any words appearing in the text in bold, **like this**,
are explained in the Glossary.

Did you know that your yard is home to lots of little creatures?

Underground

Among the plants

In the water

Which ones have you seen? Where did you see them?

Some creatures live underground. Some live among the plants. Some build nests and others live in water.

Why don't worms have legs?

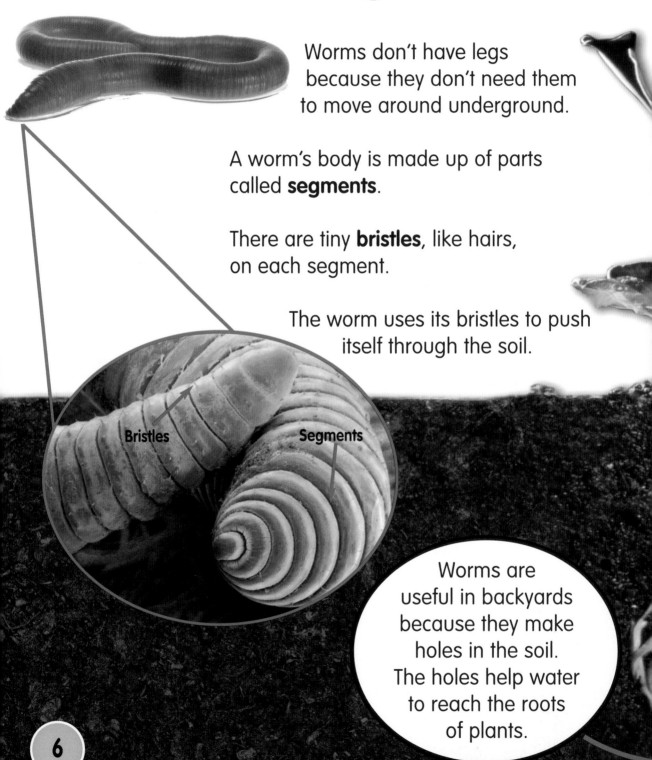

Worms don't have legs because they don't need them to move around underground.

A worm's body is made up of parts called **segments**.

There are tiny **bristles**, like hairs, on each segment.

The worm uses its bristles to push itself through the soil.

Bristles

Segments

Worms are useful in backyards because they make holes in the soil. The holes help water to reach the roots of plants.

Birds like to eat worms.

How does a spider make its web?

A spider makes its web from the threads of **silk** it makes in its body.

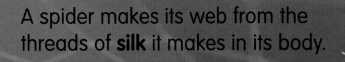

The silk is very strong, but it is very, very thin!

The spider starts with just one thread between two twigs.

Then it makes another thread. It fixes this to another twig.

It makes a shape like the **spokes** of a wheel.

Then it fills the spaces between the spokes.

Different kinds of spiders make different webs.

This kind is called an **orb web**. It is the most common type of spider web.

This kind is called a **funnel web**. The spider hides in the funnel, waiting to attack.

Spiders help gardeners. Their webs trap **insect pests** such as flies.

Trapped fly

What does a caterpillar turn into?

Caterpillars are round and long like worms, but caterpillars have legs.

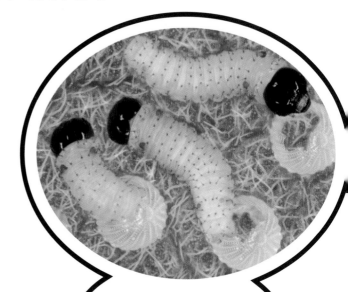

Caterpillars hatch from tiny eggs.

Each caterpillar eats lots of leaves and grows too big for its skin.

The caterpillar grows a new skin. Then its old skin falls off.

The caterpillar grows a new skin several times.

Caterpillar   **Old skin**

Pupa

After a while the caterpillar makes a shell for itself. Now it is called a **pupa**.

Something amazing happens inside the pupa. Look what comes out!

It's a butterfly!

Which insect makes honey?

Insects called bees make honey. Worker bees collect **nectar** from flowers.

Hive

They turn it into honey inside their bodies.

Bees do a dance to show each other where the flowers are.

In the hive the bees keep their honey in a honeycomb.

Young bees live in the honeycomb. They are called **larvae**.

Worker bees feed the larvae honey.

Honeycomb

Larvae

Beekeeper

Worker bee

Beekeepers collect honey from honeycombs.

13

What do ants do all day?

Ants work hard all day looking after their nest.

Some ants are soldiers. They defend the nest.

Most ants are workers. Some look after the eggs.

The queen ant lays eggs in the nest.

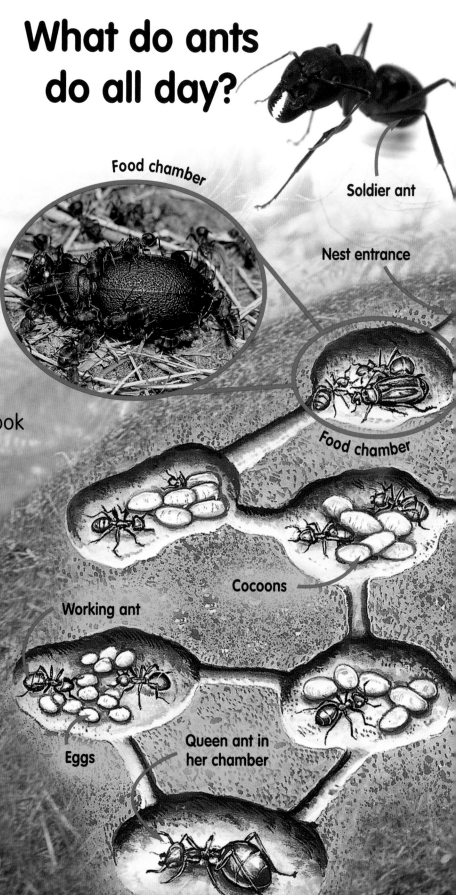

Food chamber

Soldier ant

Nest entrance

Food chamber

Cocoons

Working ant

Eggs

Queen ant in her chamber

Young ants are also called larvae.
They hatch from eggs. Workers
bring food for the larvae.

The larvae
make **cocoons**.
Inside the cocoons,
they turn into
adult ants.

Cocoons

Rubbish is
kept here

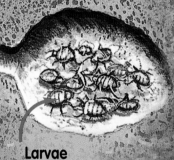

Larvae

What does a baby frog look like?

Baby frogs look a bit like fish.
They are called tadpoles.

The tadpoles start life as tiny
dots in a lump of clear jelly.
This is called **frogspawn**.

Tadpoles hatch out of the
frogspawn.

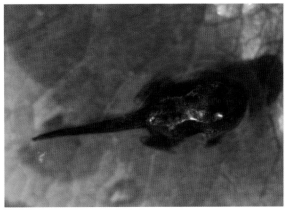

As the tadpoles grow bigger, they change shape.

They grow legs. Their tails get smaller, then disappear.

After four months, the tadpoles have changed into frogs.

Animals with lives like frogs are called **amphibians**. Newts, toads, and salamanders are also amphibians.

Why do gardeners like ladybugs?

Ladybugs are a kind of **beetle**. Most are red with black spots.

Aphids

Ladybugs are helpful in the backyard because they eat insects called **aphids**. Aphids damage plants.

If there are lots of ladybugs in your backyard, they will eat lots of aphids and the plants will grow well.

Ladybugs lay eggs.
Ladybug larvae hatch out.

Ladybug eggs

The larvae eat lots of
aphids and grow bigger.
One day they will become
adult ladybugs.

There are many
different kinds
of ladybugs.

How do snails move around?

A snail has a foot under its body. It moves around by using this foot to push itself along.

Snail foot

A snail makes slime called mucus. This helps it slide along.

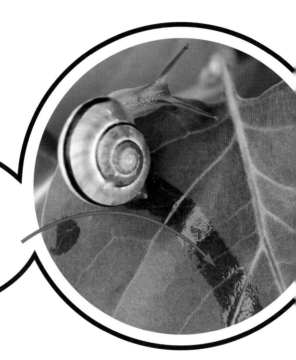

You can see where a snail has been by its trail.

Snail shell

The snail can hide inside its shell when it is afraid or when it is very hot outside.

Snails eat lots of vegetables and fruit.

Toad

But there are animals that eat snails.

Snakes, rats, frogs, and toads all eat snails. So do some birds and **beetles**.

Rat

21

Questions and answers

Q Can frogs live in and out of water?

A Yes. Animals that can do this are called amphibians.

Q How many aphids can a ladybug eat in one day?

A Ladybugs can eat 50 aphids in just one day.

Q What food do worker ants feed ant larvae?

A Ants feed their larvae on **honeydew**, a sweet liquid made by aphids.

Q Can worms see?

A No, they don't have eyes, or even a head. They can feel when things touch them.

Q What do caterpillars eat?

A Caterpillars eat the leaves of lots of different plants.

Q How fast can snails travel?

A Snails travel very slowly—it takes them an hour to travel 60 feet (18 meters).

Q Which is strongest—steel wire or spider's silk?

A A thread of spider's silk is as strong as a piece of steel wire of the same thickness.

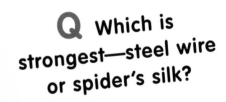

Q What do beekeepers do with the honey they collect?

A Beekeepers sell the honey for people to eat.

23

Glossary

Amphibians Animals that can live in water and on land. Frogs, toads, newts, and salamanders are all different kinds of amphibians.

Aphids Small insects that suck the juices out of plants. Other names for them are greenflies (if they are green), or blackflies (if they are black).

Beetle An insect with a hard, shiny covering over its wings.

Bristles Short, stiff hairs.

Cocoons Cases made by insects from silk that comes from inside their bodies. Inside its cocoon the insect is at the stage in its life called a pupa. This is when it changes from a young insect to a grown-up one.

Frogspawn Frogs' eggs. They look like clear jelly with the young tadpole growing inside. Toads lay the same kind of eggs.

Funnel web A funnel web is a spider's web that is the shape of a funnel.

Honeydew A liquid made in the bodies of aphids. Aphids suck the juice from plants and pass it out of their bodies as sweet honeydew.

Insects Animals that have six legs and a body in three parts. There are thousands of different kinds of insects in the world.

Larvae The young of many kinds of insects are called larvae. Caterpillars are the larvae of butterflies.

Nectar A sweet liquid found inside flowers.

Orb web An orb web is a spider's web that is the shape of a circle.

Pests Animals that do damage to plants.

Pupa An insect that is changing into an adult.

Segments Parts of something.

Silk Fine thread produced by spiders from inside their bodies. They use it to make webs. Some insects also make silk.

Spokes The bits of a wheel that stick out from the middle to the edge.

Index